inside the HUMAN body

By Steve Parker

Illustrated by Alex Pang

Miles Kelly

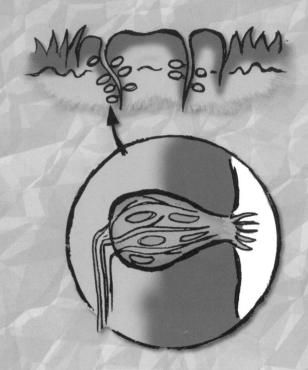

ACKNOWLEDGEMENTS

All panel artworks by Rocket Design

The publishers would like to thank the following sources for the use of their photographs:

Front cover: Fotolia: (c)York
Back cover: Shutterstock: (c)beerkoff
Getty Images: 32(b) MCT
Rex Features: 7(cr) Sipa Press
Shutterstock: COVER Ljupco Smokovski, Taranova; 6(c) muzsy,(b) Triff; 8 Monkey Business Images; 10 Vishal Shah; 12 Taranova; 14 bezikus; 16 JonMilnes; 18 beerkoff; 20 Daniel Rajszczak; 22 paul Prescott; 24 Picsfive; 30 Remzi; 33(br) Alex Luengo; 35 Oleinikova Olga; 36 Patricia Marroquin Science
Photo Library: 7(b) SIU; 27 Dr P. Marazzi; 29 Simon Fraser/ NCCT, Freeman Trust Newcastle-Upon-Tyne; 32 AJ Photo

All other photographs are from Miles Kelly Archives

WWW.FACTSFORPROJECTS.COM

Each top right-hand page directs you to the Internet to help you find out more. You can log on to **www.factsforprojects.com** to find free pictures, additional information, videos, fun activities and further web links. These are for your own personal use and should not be copied or distributed for any commercial or profit-related purpose.

If you do decide to use the Internet with your book, here's a list of what you'll need:
• A PC with Microsoft® Windows® XP or later versions, or a Macintosh with OS X or later, and 512Mb RAM

• A browser such as Microsoft® Internet Explorer 9, Firefox 4.X or Safari 5.X
• Connection to the Internet. Broadband connection recommended
• An account with an Internet Service Provider (ISP)
• A sound card for listening to sound files

Links won't work?
www.factsforprojects.com is regularly checked to make sure the links provide you with lots of information. Sometimes you may receive a message saying that a site is unavailable. If this happens, just try again later.

Stay safe!
When using the Internet, make sure you follow these guidelines:
• Ask a parent's or a guardian's permission before you log on.
• Never give out your personal details, such as your name, address or email.
• If a site asks you to log in or register by typing your name or email address, speak to your parent or guardian first.
• If you do receive an email from someone you don't know, tell an adult and do not reply to the message.
• Never arrange to meet anyone you have talked to on the Internet.

Miles Kelly Publishing is not responsible for the accuracy or suitability of the information on any website other than its own. We recommend that children are supervised while on the Internet and that they do not use Internet chat rooms.

www.mileskelly.net

info@mileskelly.net

CONTENTS

INTRODUCTION

The human body is perhaps the most studied object in the world. As well as being endlessly fascinating, it contains a dozen main systems that are vital for our survival. Each system is comprised of many parts – organs and tissues – working together to carry out an important function, such as breathing or digestion. The more we know about how the body works, the better each of us can care for our own personal, amazing, natural machine.

More than four new human bodies enter the world every second – and two die.

UNDER THE SKIN

The body's biggest single organ – the skin – is visible for all to see. Like many other organs, it has several tasks. Skin covers, protects, helps control temperature, and senses touch. The next biggest organ is the liver, in the right side of the torso. It has hundreds of jobs, adjusting levels of blood sugar, minerals and nutrients. Co-ordinating all these parts, and more, is the brain. It receives and sends millions of tiny electrical nerve signals every second through the network of billions of nerve cells.

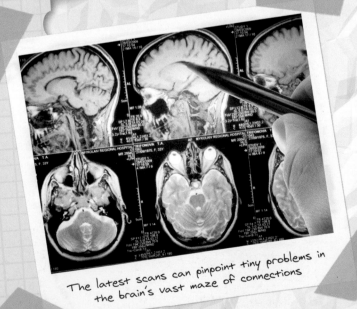

Top athletes combine supreme physical skill, focused determination and dedicated practise to achieve results.

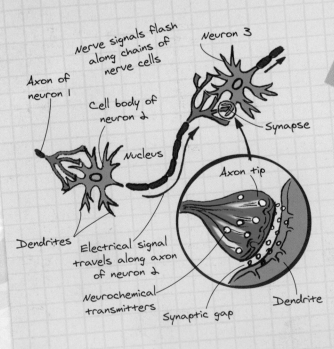

Nerve signals flash along chains of nerve cells

Neuron 3

Axon of neuron 1

Cell body of neuron 2

Synapse

Nucleus

Axon tip

Dendrites

Electrical signal travels along axon of neuron 2

Neurochemical transmitters

Synaptic gap

Dendrite

The latest scans can pinpoint tiny problems in the brain's vast maze of connections

The topics featured in this book are Internet linked.
Visit www.factsforprojects.com to find out more.

MECHANICAL MARVEL

The human body is a mechanical masterpiece capable of incredible feats of strength and movement. At a basic level, our muscles pull bones to move them at joints. It sounds simple, but for each muscle contraction that takes place, dozens of other muscles work to steady the other parts around it, adjust the body's posture, and keep it well balanced. This involves thousands of nerve signals every second passing from the brain's movement centres out to the muscles. There is feedback too, from sensors in the muscles, tendons and skin, and from the eyes, so the brain knows how the movement is progressing.

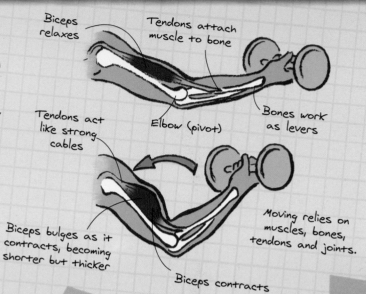

Biceps relaxes

Tendons attach muscle to bone

Tendons act like strong cables

Elbow (pivot)

Bones work as levers

Biceps bulges as it contracts, becoming shorter but thicker

Moving relies on muscles, bones, tendons and joints.

Biceps contracts

Using microscopes, surgeons can perform operations on nerves thinner than this 'l'.

With determination and practise, limb loss can be turned into sporting victory

MEDICAL WONDERS

Treating, healing and curing the sick or diseased body are among the greatest achievements of modern science. Every year sees new kinds of scans and diagnostic tests, better medical drugs to ease pain and suffering, and advances in surgery that seem almost miraculous. There is also the rise of genetic treatments. These aim to change the genes – the instructions for how the body develops and runs itself. In the future, gene therapies may get to the very core of how the body works, why it goes wrong, and how it can be mended.

SKIN, HAIR AND NAILS

Without its ever-renewing skin, the body's delicate inner parts and fluids would be exposed to all kinds of knocks, scrapes, dirt and germs. The skin is one of the body's busiest parts. Its outer layer, the epidermis, completely replaces itself every month to cope with constant wear and tear. It is also the biggest sense organ, responding to physical contact as well as heat, cold, vibration, pressure and pain.

Did you know?

Almost every second, even when the body is asleep, dozens of tiny, worn skin flakes fall from its surface. Towelling yourself dry after a shower removes many millions of them. If you collected all these flakes, in one year they would fill three average 10-litre buckets.

An average adult's skin has an area of about 2 sq m, which is approximately the size of a single bed.

✳ Skin deep

Skin colour comes from microscopic cells know as melanocytes dotted through the base of the epidermis. They make tiny particles of the very dark-brown pigment melanin, which they pass to other epidermal cells around them. Most people have the same number of melanocytes, about 1000 in every square millimetre of skin. The colour of skin depends on how active these cells are, which is determined by genes. Exposure to ultra-violet rays makes melanocytes more active, darkening the skin to protect against sunburn.

Sweat duct This thin tube connects the sweat gland in the dermis to the pore at the surface. Watery sweat cools the body as it dries.

Sweat pore

Almost half a litre of water is lost every day by evaporation through the epidermis and sweating.

Sebaceous gland makes sebum

Skin comes in all shades from almost white to dark brown

Hair root Hairs grow at their root, from a deep infolded pocket of the epidermis known as a hair follicle. Each follicle has a sebaceous, or skin-oil, gland.

Subcutaneous fat layer

Find out more about what skin is made of and how it can be damaged by visiting www.factsforprojects.com and clicking on the web link.

Fingernails grow about 3 mm each week, and faster in summer than winter. Toenails grow slightly more slowly.

NAILS

Nail root (growing part)

Nail is made of keratin — the same substance that is in hair

Bone

Nail bed

Hair shaft Scalp hairs grow 2–3 mm each week. Each hair grows for three to five years before it falls out and a new one starts to grow from the same follicle.

Epidermal surface

Hair shaft

Erector muscle relaxed

Skin surface (epidermis)

Layer of warm air is trapped near skin

Hair root in dermis

Erector muscles contract and make hair erect

Epidermis The upper layer of skin grows continually at its base layer. Its cells fill with the tough protein keratin, die, move up and rub away at the surface.

✳ How do HAIRS stand on end?

Humans have several million body hairs – about as many as our close mammal cousins, chimpanzees and gorillas. However ours are much shorter and finer. Even so, they still work to try and provide insulation and keep the body warm in cold conditions. The tiny muscle at the base of each hair, the erector pili, shortens to tilt the hair shaft more upright, making the hairs stand on end. This thickens the layer of air trapped next to the skin for better insulation. The muscle actions cause the skin around the hairs to pucker into small mounds known as 'goosebumps'.

Dermis The lower layer of skin contains tough fibres of collagen and stretchy strands of elastin, as well as hair follicles, sweat glands, sebaceous glands and touch sensors.

The thinnest skin is on the eyelids and lips, where it is less than 0.5 mm thick. The thickest is on the soles of the feet. In someone who rarely wears shoes it can be more than 5 mm thick.

Blood supply The dermis and subcutaneous layers are well supplied with blood by microscopic capillaries, and slightly larger arterioles (red) and venules (blue).

Erector muscle

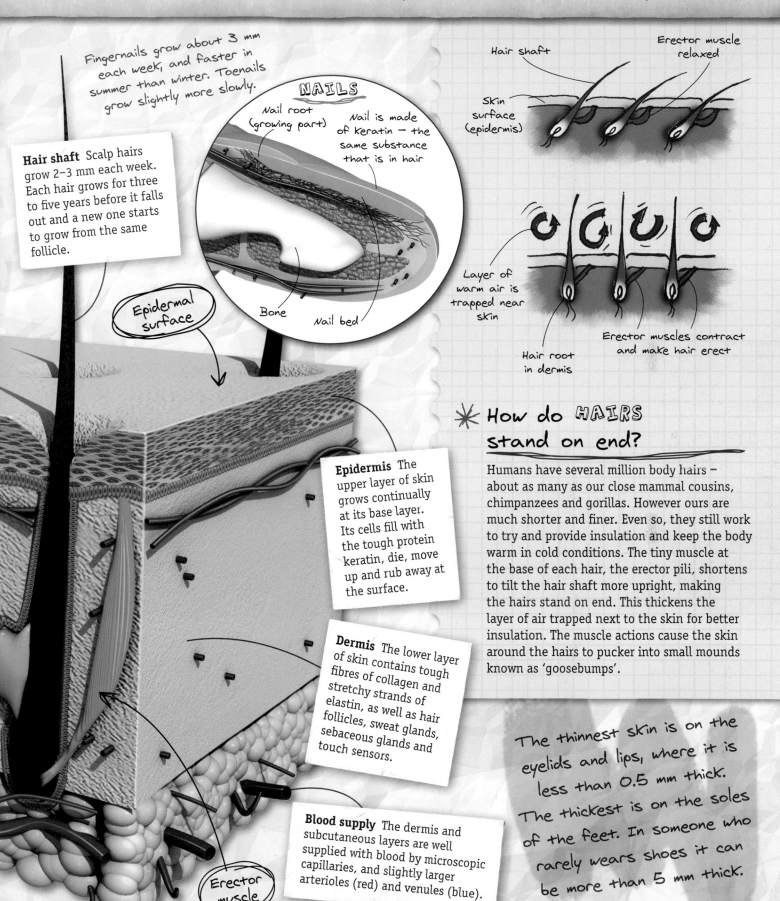

SKELETON AND BONES

The 206 bones of the skeleton are pale, shiny and very active. They continually renew their structure, replenish their mineral reserves, and repair tiny chips or cracks. Over time, bones can even respond to the body's movement patterns by adding strengthening fibres along the most recent lines of greatest stress.

Did you know?

Few parts of the body are as active as the jelly-like marrow inside most bones. This has a rich blood and nerve supply. Red marrow makes all the new cells for the blood – red blood cells are produced here at the rate of up to three million per second.

There are 22 main bones in the skull. But only one can move – the lower jaw. The others are fixed firmly together along wavy joints known as sutures.

Head The end of a long bone is known as the head. It is ball-shaped to fit and move inside its joint. It is covered by smooth cartilage, as shown on pages 14–15.

INSIDE A BONE

Most bones have a very hard, dense outer layer that provides most of the strength. Inside this is a more lightweight, honeycomb-like spongy layer. The marrow cavity is at the centre.

Bones grow and adapt to the stresses put on the body. For example, in a tennis player, they become stronger and more robust in the arm that holds the racquet.

Periosteum (outer covering)

Marrow and blood vessels

Spongy or cancellous bone

Hard or compact bone

When upright the body can support lots of extra weight

✳ MECHANICAL marvel

Unlike nearly all of our mammal relatives, the human skeleton's greatest strength is in the vertical direction. As the body's main upright support, the vertebral (spinal) column of backbones is designed to cope with being squashed or compressed in a downwards direction, since all the body parts 'hang' from it. If we stay fairly upright, we can carry quite heavy loads. But bending or leaning in the wrong way, or for too long, puts huge extra stresses on the spine and causes backache and injury.

Most bones are in the extremities (the hands and feet). Each wrist has 8, then 5 in the palm and 14 in the thumb and fingers. The ankle has 7, with again 5 in the foot and 14 in the toes.

Learn the names of the bones in your body and test yourself on an interactive skeleton by visiting www.factsforprojects.com and clicking on the web link.

Mandible (lower jaw)

SKELETON

Chest The 12 pairs of ribs protect the heart and lungs. The top seven pairs ('true ribs') join to the sternum. The next three pairs ('false ribs') attach to the lowest of the true ribs. The bottom two pairs ('floating ribs') attach only to the spine.

Spine There are 33 vertebrae, or backbones, in the spinal column. Most of them can move slightly against their neighbours to give overall flexibility.

Carpal (wrist) bones

Leg bones The femur (thigh bone) connects to the tibia and fibula bones of the lower leg at a complex knee joint. The tibia, or shinbone, is sturdier than the slender fibula.

Patella (kneecap)

The bones of the ankle are called tarsal bones.

Ankle The hard, bony lumps on the outside and inside of the ankle region are not true ankle (tarsal) bones. They are the outward-projecting bases of the fibula and tibia in the lower leg.

The bulkiest bone is the pelvis (hip bone). The femur (thigh bone) is the longest, and makes up one-quarter of the body's height. The smallest is the stirrup, deep in the ear.

Bones may seem hard and dry, but they are on average one-fifth water.

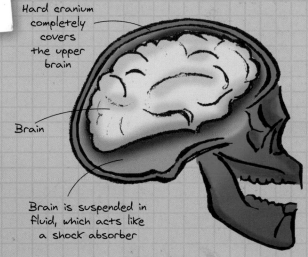

Hard cranium completely covers the upper brain

Brain

Brain is suspended in fluid, which acts like a shock absorber

✳ How do BONES protect you?

Bones offer protection as well as support. The delicate brain is completely surrounded by the bones of the skull. Above the brain is the dome of the cranium, formed from eight large, curved, bony plates. Its curved shape provides great strength to resist knocks and pressure. Below the brain are the 14 bones of the face and cranial floor. For added protection, we have skin and hair on the outside, and on the inside is a liquid called cerebrospinal fluid. This surrounds the brain so it 'floats' and is cushioned against impact. In the hip region, the curved, flared, bowl-shaped pelvis cradles and protects the parts inside the lower body, including the bladder and the female reproductive organs.

MUSCLES AND MOVEMENT

In relatively fit people who are not overweight, muscles make up about two-fifths of body weight. Despite this bulk, and compared to many other multi-tasking parts of the body, muscles have just one main function – to shorten, or contract. With more than 640 muscles to control, the brain learns to make most movements and actions almost automatically.

Did you know?

People who are very fit and strong do not have more muscles. Everyone has the same number. However their individual muscles can develop bigger muscle fibres for greater strength and an improved blood flow bringing more oxygen and energy.

The most powerful muscles for their size are the temporalis and masseter, the main jaw muscles.

Fascicle Myofibres are about as thin as hairs. A bundle of myofibres is called a fascicle.

INSIDE A MUSCLE

Group of fascicles (bundles)

Body of muscle The main body, or belly, contains many bundles of muscle fibres. Each of these fascicles is wrapped in a sheath, the perimysium. Around the whole muscle is a covering called the epimysium.

Myofibrils Each myofibre (muscle fibre) is composed of many even thinner myofibrils (muscle filaments), where contraction is based.

✳ MUSCLE pumping

Several main types of myofibril (muscle filaments) make up muscle fibres. FT (fast twitch) fibres contract quickly and powerfully, but they soon run out of energy and become fatigued rapidly. ST (slow twitch) fibres take longer to shorten, and do so less powerfully, but they can keep going for longer. Every muscle in each person has its own mix of ST and FT fibres. The proportions are possessed from birth and partly determine whether that person will be good at 'explosive' actions such as weightlifting or long-jump, or longer-term, high-stamina activities such as distance running.

The more we use our muscles, the stronger they become

Tiny muscles, such as those inside the inner ear, have just a few dozen muscle fibres. Big muscles in the leg have many thousands.

Muscles are controlled by nerve signals coming from the brain along motor nerves.

Discover more about the muscular system by visiting www.factsforprojects.com and clicking on the web link.

MUSCLES OF THE BODY

Jaw muscles

Pectoralis

Abdominal muscles
There are three main layers of abdominal muscles, often called 'abs'. These give strength to the front of the abdomen, where there are no bones.

Tendons pass through wrist

As well as skeletal (striped) muscles that move bones, there are also visceral (smooth) muscles in the guts, bladder and other inner organs, and cardiac muscle in the heart.

Tendon connects muscle to bone

Tibialis anterior muscle

Muscles of the femur
Four large, powerful muscles at the front of the thigh, known as the quadriceps femoris, bend the hip to pull the thigh up and forwards, and also straighten the knee.

Gastrocnemius

Ankle tendons
Tendons from muscles in the lower leg pass through the ankle to pull the foot and toe bones. The wrist has a similar arrangement between the forearm muscles and fingers.

✳ How do MUSCLES work?

The long bones of the arms and legs are the body's mechanical levers. Their joints, such as the shoulder, elbow, hip and knee, are the mechanical versions of pivots. When a muscle such as the biceps muscle in the upper arm contracts, it pulls the lower arm bone near the elbow joint. The biceps may only shorten by a few centimetres, but since its point of attachment is so near the elbow, it moves the lower arm bones to swing the hand through an arc of many centimetres. In engineering, this extra movement is known as mechanical advantage.

Biceps relaxes

Tendons attach muscle to bone

Tendons act like strong cables

Elbow (pivot)

Bones work as levers

Biceps contracts

Biceps bulges as it contracts, becoming shorter but thicker

The bulkiest muscle in the body is the gluteus maximus in the buttock and upper rear thigh. It pulls the thigh backwards when walking, running and jumping.

The body's smallest muscle is the tiny stapedius, attached to the stirrup bone in the ear (see page 32–33).

JOINTS

Individual bones are just one part of the skeletal system. For bones to move, they must be linked at joints. There are more than 300 joints in the body, varying from the largest single joint, the knee, to the smallest, the knuckles. In a joint, bone is covered by smooth cartilage and lubricated by fluid. Each joint is purpose-designed in shape and size to allow enough movement in certain directions, but without too much freedom, which would diminish strength and stability.

Did you know?

Tiny amounts of thick, slimy synovial fluid are found in joints. Each knee – the biggest joint – has less than a teaspoon of this. If the synovial fluid was collected from all the body's joints, it would hardly half-fill a coffee mug.

✳ BENT double

Joints that are well used stay flexible and smooth-moving for many years. This is partly due to the muscles that work them keeping their strength and so preventing a joint from over-flexing, which causes tears and swelling. However, too much use, and especially unnatural actions such as twisting that are necessary in certain sports, can build up many small areas of damage. These can develop into joint problems such as osteoarthritis.

Saddle joint The base of the thumb has a saddle joint, like two horse saddles against each other. This allows tilting and sliding.

TYPES OF JOINTS

Ball-and-socket joints allow bones to rotate in all directions, creating a range of movements. Hinge joints only allow movement forwards and backwards.

Compound joints such as the jaw can move from front to back, and side to side, but cannot rotate.

Jaw (compound)

Shoulder (ball-and-socket)

Elbow (hinge)

Fingers (hinges)

Hip (ball-and-socket)

Knee (hinge)

The smallest joints are between the smallest bones — the hammer, anvil and stirrup inside the ear.

Ankle (compound)

The most flexible joints are also the least stable. Both the shoulder and hip are ball-and-socket designs. But the shoulder is much more flexible, making it more likely to dislocate or 'pop out'.

Ballet dancers work to become incredibly flexible yet strong

To test your knowledge of the joints in your skeleton and their locations visit www.factsforprojects.com and click on the web link.

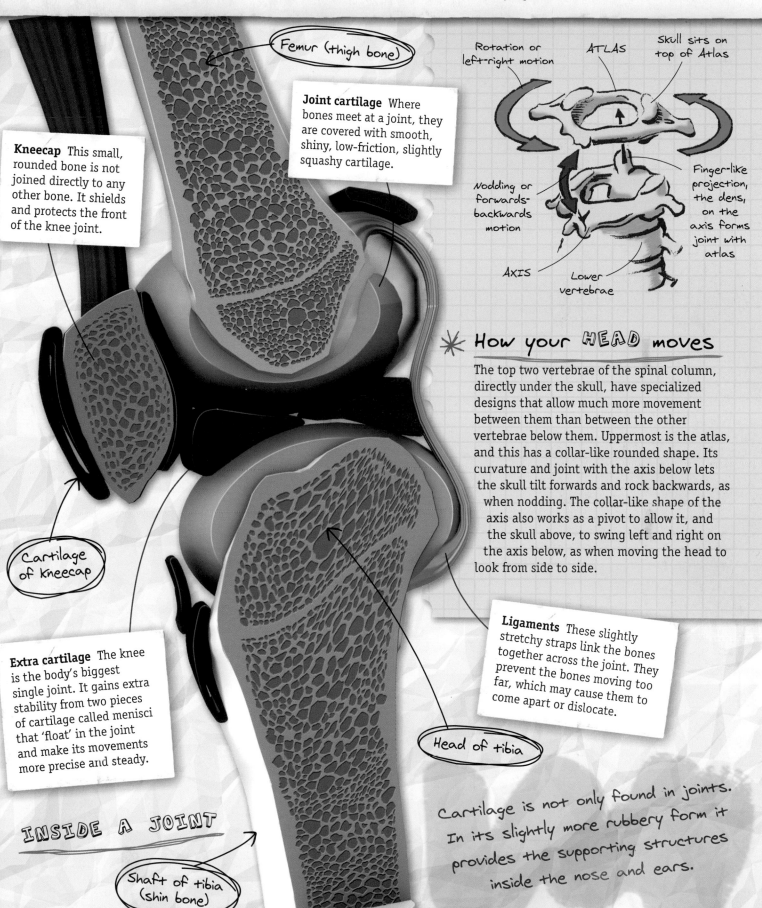

Femur (thigh bone)

Joint cartilage Where bones meet at a joint, they are covered with smooth, shiny, low-friction, slightly squashy cartilage.

Kneecap This small, rounded bone is not joined directly to any other bone. It shields and protects the front of the knee joint.

Rotation or left-right motion

ATLAS

Skull sits on top of Atlas

Nodding or forwards-backwards motion

Finger-like projection, the dens, on the axis forms joint with atlas

AXIS

Lower vertebrae

✳ How your HEAD moves

The top two vertebrae of the spinal column, directly under the skull, have specialized designs that allow much more movement between them than between the other vertebrae below them. Uppermost is the atlas, and this has a collar-like rounded shape. Its curvature and joint with the axis below lets the skull tilt forwards and rock backwards, as when nodding. The collar-like shape of the axis also works as a pivot to allow it, and the skull above, to swing left and right on the axis below, as when moving the head to look from side to side.

Cartilage of kneecap

Extra cartilage The knee is the body's biggest single joint. It gains extra stability from two pieces of cartilage called menisci that 'float' in the joint and make its movements more precise and steady.

Ligaments These slightly stretchy straps link the bones together across the joint. They prevent the bones moving too far, which may cause them to come apart or dislocate.

Head of tibia

INSIDE A JOINT

Shaft of tibia (shin bone)

Cartilage is not only found in joints. In its slightly more rubbery form it provides the supporting structures inside the nose and ears.

LUNGS AND BREATHING

The body can last for days without food, and even a day or two without water. But without oxygen from the air, its cells and tissues start to die within minutes. The lungs are the vital organs that take oxygen from air and pass it to the bloodstream. They do the equally important task of getting rid of the waste product carbon dioxide. If this builds up in the body, it could kill even faster than a lack of oxygen.

Did you know?

If all of the airways in the body were joined end to end, from the main windpipe to the tiniest bronchioles, they would stretch more than 50 kilometres. From the windpipe to the air sacs (alveoli) is about 15 branchings.

In both lungs, there are more than 300 million tiny air chambers called alveoli. They provide a tennis-court-sized area for taking in oxygen and getting rid of waste carbon dioxide.

The branching airways, from the windpipe to the main bronchi, then smaller bronchi and bronchioles, are known as the 'respiratory tree'.

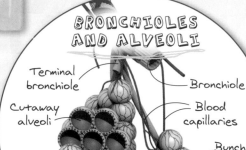

BRONCHIOLES AND ALVEOLI

Terminal bronchiole

Bronchiole

Cutaway alveoli

Blood capillaries

Bunch of alveoli

✳ PHEW!

Stored air in bottles or tanks allows humans to travel to, and work in, all kinds of hazardous environments where otherwise we would soon suffocate – die from lack of oxygen. These places include under the water, deep mines and caverns, wells, swamps and volcanoes. Here gases such as methane and carbon dioxide would otherwise poison the body. Breathing apparatus is especially important for firefighters since the air around them is smoke-laden, lacking in oxygen, and also so hot it would burn the airways.

Deep in the lungs The smallest airways – bronchioles – are thinner than hairs. They lead to bunches of microscopic bubble-like air chambers called alveoli, where oxygen passes into the blood.

At rest, most people breathe 12–15 times each minute.

Blood system Pulmonary (lung) arteries (blue) bring stale blood from the heart. After this is refreshed with oxygen it goes back to the heart along pulmonary veins (red).

Diaphragm This muscle sheet works under instructions from the brain's automatic breathing or respiratory centre.

The stale air from a scuba diver's lungs bubbles into the water

To see an animated diagram of how breathing works visit www.factsforprojects.com and click on the web link.

Air from a sneeze travels at more than 200 km/h.

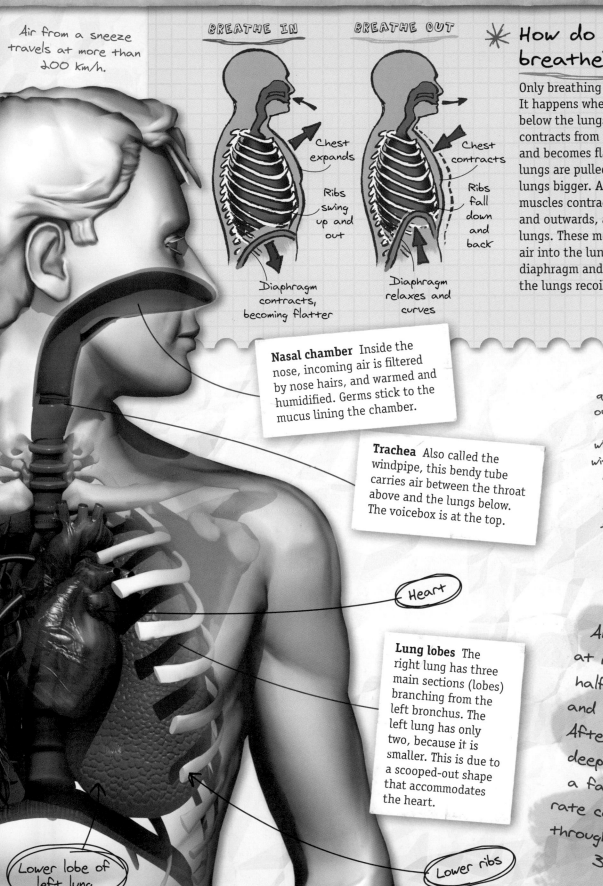

BREATHE IN

Chest expands

Ribs swing up and out

Diaphragm contracts, becoming flatter

BREATHE OUT

Chest contracts

Ribs fall down and back

Diaphragm relaxes and curves

How do LUNGS breathe?

Only breathing in is muscle-powered. It happens when the sheet of muscle below the lungs, called the diaphragm, contracts from its relaxed dome shape and becomes flatter. The bases of the lungs are pulled down, making the lungs bigger. At the same time, rib muscles contract to make them tilt up and outwards, again stretching the lungs. These movements suck fresh air into the lungs. To breathe out, the diaphragm and rib muscles relax and the lungs recoil to their smaller size.

Nasal chamber Inside the nose, incoming air is filtered by nose hairs, and warmed and humidified. Germs stick to the mucus lining the chamber.

Trachea Also called the windpipe, this bendy tube carries air between the throat above and the lungs below. The voicebox is at the top.

Heart

Lung lobes The right lung has three main sections (lobes) branching from the left bronchus. The left lung has only two, because it is smaller. This is due to a scooped-out shape that accommodates the heart.

When we speak quietly, we breathe out up to ten times more slowly than when we breathe out without speaking. The air passes between two ridges — the vocal cords — inside the voicebox (larynx). This flow makes the cords vibrate to produce sounds.

An average breath at rest moves around half a litre of air in and out of the lungs. After great activity, deeper breaths and a faster breathing rate can increase the throughflow of air by 30 times.

Lower lobe of left lung

Lower ribs

HEART AND BLOOD

The heart is not much more than a simple blood pump. However, it is an amazingly reliable and efficient one, beating perhaps three billion times during a lifetime. The heart is also very responsive in its speed and output. During great activity it can pump more than seven times the amount of blood than it does when the body is at rest.

Did you know?

The distribution of blood around the body is very 'one-sided'. At any moment about three-quarters is in the veins, on the way back to the heart. One-fifth is in the arteries and only one-twentieth is in the capillary network.

An average adult human body contains between 4 and 5 litres of blood.

Superior vena cava

Pulmonary arteries

Right atrium Each upper small chamber, the atrium, has thin, floppy walls. It receives blood from the veins and squeezes to push it through the atrio-ventricular valve to the ventricle below.

Heart wall The walls of the heart are made of cardiac muscle. Unlike skeletal muscles, this can work non-stop without tiring.

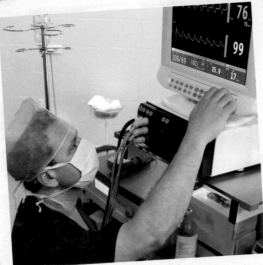

The electrocardiogram (ECG) machine records heartbeats

✳ Tick TOCK Tick TOCK

The heart has many litres of blood passing through it every minute. But it cannot use this blood for its own supplies of oxygen, energy and nutrients for the ever-demanding muscles in its walls. Blood within the heart undergoes waves of very high pressure and fast movement, which would burst delicate capillaries. Also blood in the right side of the heart is low in oxygen. So there are specialized vessels called coronary arteries, which convey fresh, high-oxygen blood from near the start of the aorta (main artery) and branch to distribute it to the heart muscles.

LOCATION

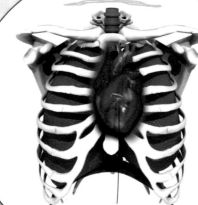

Two-thirds of the heart is on the left side of the body

Right ventricle The thick-walled, muscular lower chamber pumps low-oxygen blood out to the lungs.

Inferior vena cava

Watch a heart beating and find out why heart attacks happen by visiting www.factsforprojects.com and clicking on the web link.

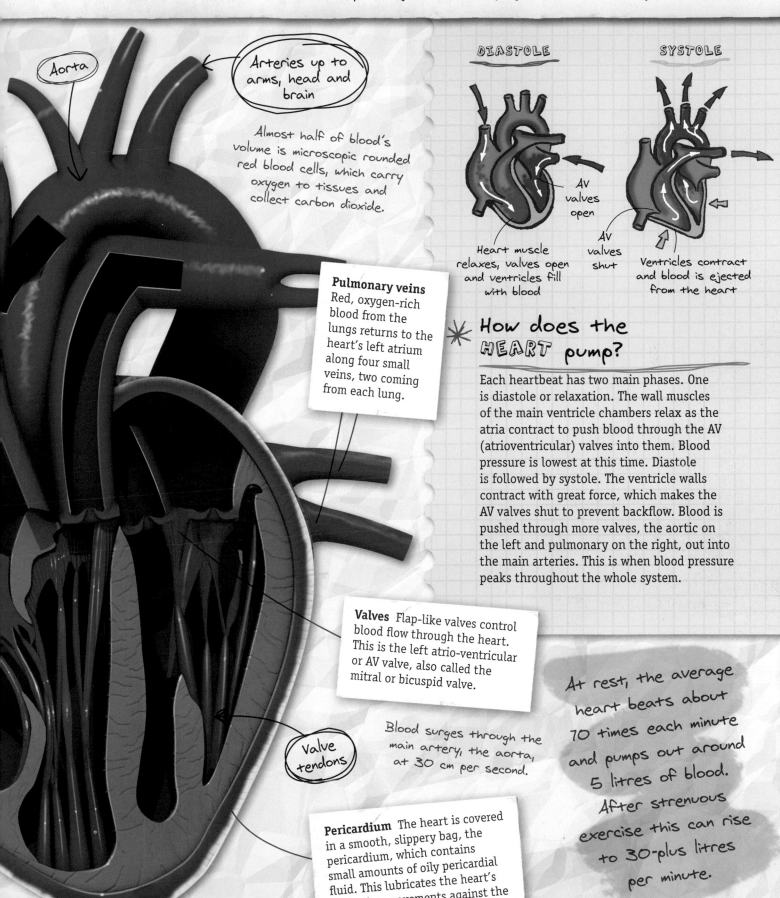

Aorta

Arteries up to arms, head and brain

Almost half of blood's volume is microscopic rounded red blood cells, which carry oxygen to tissues and collect carbon dioxide.

DIASTOLE

SYSTOLE

AV valves open

Heart muscle relaxes, valves open and ventricles fill with blood

AV valves shut

Ventricles contract and blood is ejected from the heart

Pulmonary veins
Red, oxygen-rich blood from the lungs returns to the heart's left atrium along four small veins, two coming from each lung.

How does the HEART pump?

Each heartbeat has two main phases. One is diastole or relaxation. The wall muscles of the main ventricle chambers relax as the atria contract to push blood through the AV (atrioventricular) valves into them. Blood pressure is lowest at this time. Diastole is followed by systole. The ventricle walls contract with great force, which makes the AV valves shut to prevent backflow. Blood is pushed through more valves, the aortic on the left and pulmonary on the right, out into the main arteries. This is when blood pressure peaks throughout the whole system.

Valves Flap-like valves control blood flow through the heart. This is the left atrio-ventricular or AV valve, also called the mitral or bicuspid valve.

Blood surges through the main artery, the aorta, at 30 cm per second.

Valve tendons

At rest, the average heart beats about 70 times each minute and pumps out around 5 litres of blood. After strenuous exercise this can rise to 30-plus litres per minute.

Pericardium The heart is covered in a smooth, slippery bag, the pericardium, which contains small amounts of oily pericardial fluid. This lubricates the heart's squirming movements against the body parts around it.

TEETH

As well as being covered with the body's hardest substance, enamel, teeth have the shortest growing time of almost any body part. Adult or permanent (second-set) teeth take several months to enlarge from tiny buds to their full size, from the ages of about six to 18 years, depending on their position in the mouth. Then they hardly enlarge at all – for what could be 100 years.

Did you know?

The adult set of teeth is supposed to number 32. The rearmost four molars or cheek teeth – left and right, in upper and lower jaws – are called wisdom teeth. But in about one person in three, the wisdom teeth never erupt, or develop enough to show above the gum.

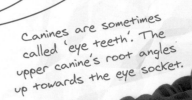

Ancient Romans carved false teeth for people in ivory – from the teeth of elephants.

✳ OPEN WIDE!

Over thousands of years, average human jaws have become smaller, while the teeth have done so at a lesser rate. This means many people have crowded teeth, or the teeth grow crooked as they try to force their way into too small gaps between their neighbours. Various kinds of dental appliances or 'braces' help to make sure the teeth grow straight and even. This not only improves their appearance, but also makes them easier to clean and evens out the pressures on them during eating.

Incisor teeth The eight incisors are in two sets of four in the upper and lower jaws. They have straight, sharp edges, like small chisels, and are suited to nibbling and gnawing.

Canines are sometimes called 'eye teeth'. The upper canine's root angles up towards the eye socket.

Canine teeth There are four canines, two upper and two lower, each behind the incisors. These tall, pointed teeth are adapted to tear and rip up chunks of food.

As the body ages, the gums start to shrink or recede to expose more root and make the crown appear longer, hence the saying 'long in the tooth'.

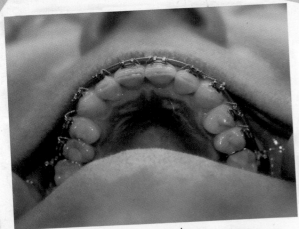

Dental braces help teeth to grow straight and evenly-spaced

Crown and root Each tooth has a crown visible above the gum and a root that anchors it into the jawbone. The crown and root meet at the gum line which is known as the neck of the tooth. The crown is covered by enamel.

Arch-shaped lower jaw or mandible

For some fun facts about teeth visit
www.factsforprojects.com and click on the web link.

The pulp contains nerves that warn of too
much pressure, which might crack the tooth.

Gums The gum or gingival tissue is soft but hard-wearing, and very active. It replaces itself rapidly as eating wears it away.

Incisors and canines usually have one root. But premolars and molars often have two, perhaps three, or even more. Each person's tooth anatomy is as individual as fingerprints.

Premolars In each side (left and right) of each jaw (upper and lower) are two premolar teeth. They help the molars with crushing and chewing and also have a shear-like action.

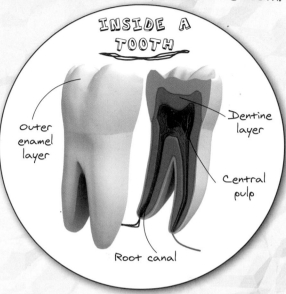

INSIDE A TOOTH

Outer enamel layer

Dentine layer

Central pulp

Root canal

Molars At the rear of the jaw on either side are three molar teeth. They are broad with cusps (points) for powerful chewing.

Double-rooted first molar

Unless it is very yellow, pitted and decaying, the colour of enamel does not indicate its hardness.

Jawbone The tooth root is fixed almost rigidly into the jaw with a living form of cement plus strong periodontal fibres.

✳ How do TEETH grow?

Well before birth, the beginnings of two sets of teeth are formed inside the jaw bone. The first of the 20 baby, milk or deciduous teeth appear or 'erupt' on average after 6–9 months, and all of them have grown by three years. The adult or permanent teeth then start to replace them from around six to seven years of age, pushing out the first teeth as they grow. By the age of 20 years, all of the adult teeth have appeared – except perhaps for the wisdom teeth (see opposite).

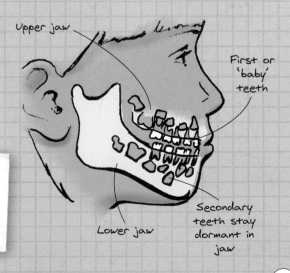

Upper jaw

First or 'baby' teeth

Lower jaw

Secondary teeth stay dormant in jaw

DIGESTIVE SYSTEM

A typical person eats more than half a tonne of food each year – about ten times the body's entire weight. Food is not just nutrients and raw materials for growth and repair of wear and tear. It also brings high-energy substances, especially sugars and starches, and to some extent fats, that provide the power for life processes, keeping warm and moving about.

Did you know?

The human digestive tract, from mouth to anus, is usually said to be about 9 metres in length. However, this is when its wall muscles are relaxed and floppy, which is usually after death. When the muscles are tensed and working, the tract is nearer 5–6 metres.

Chewing food makes it soft and easy to swallow, starts its physical breakdown, and also mixes it with saliva, which begins its chemical breakdown.

✳ Healthy GUTS

Some of the most important foods we eat give very little nutrition and energy, yet they are vital for healthy digestion. They contain plenty of fibre or 'roughage'. Our digestive system cannot break this down, but fibre gives the food bulk so that it can be gripped and moved easily through the system. It also absorbs various unwanted substances which could otherwise cause damage, and protects against problems such as certain forms of cancer. Fresh fruits and vegetables are the best sources of fibre, and we should aim to eat at least 'five a day'.

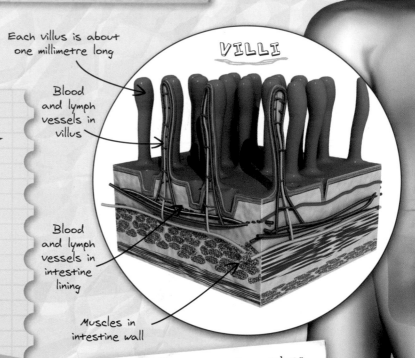

VILLI

Each villus is about one millimetre long

Blood and lymph vessels in villus

Blood and lymph vessels in intestine lining

Muscles in intestine wall

Small intestine and villi The very long, but narrow and winding, small intestine has millions of tiny finger-shaped villi inside. These greatly increase the surface area for absorbing digested food.

Ascending colon

Colon The large intestine or colon forms a 'frame' around the small intestine. It absorbs water and minerals, and compresses the wastes for removal.

Fruit and vegetables are essential to keep our bodies healthy

Find more amazing facts, pictures and videos about the digestive system by visiting www.factsforprojects.com and clicking on the web link.

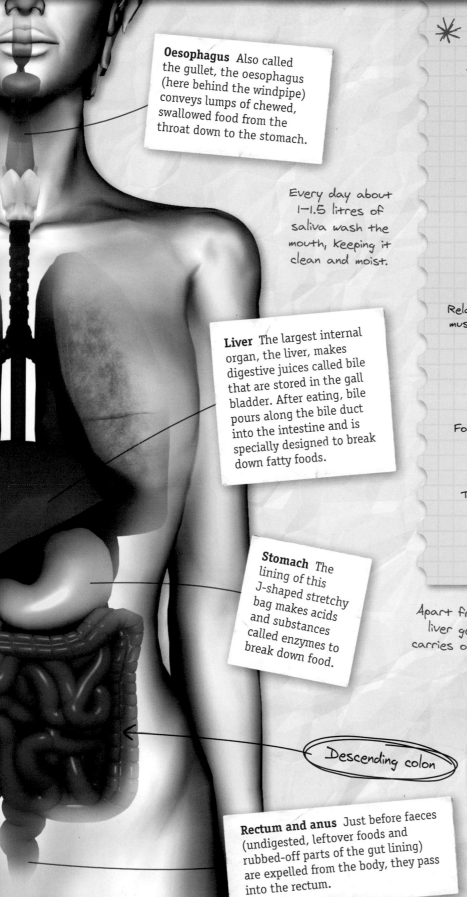

Oesophagus Also called the gullet, the oesophagus (here behind the windpipe) conveys lumps of chewed, swallowed food from the throat down to the stomach.

Every day about 1–1.5 litres of saliva wash the mouth, keeping it clean and moist.

Liver The largest internal organ, the liver, makes digestive juices called bile that are stored in the gall bladder. After eating, bile pours along the bile duct into the intestine and is specially designed to break down fatty foods.

Stomach The lining of this J-shaped stretchy bag makes acids and substances called enzymes to break down food.

Descending colon

Rectum and anus Just before faeces (undigested, leftover foods and rubbed-off parts of the gut lining) are expelled from the body, they pass into the rectum.

✳ How does PERISTALSIS work?

Peristalsis is the wave-like contraction of muscles all along the walls of the gut or digestive tract. It begins when food enters the oesophagus, and ends when leftover wastes come out of the anus. Circular muscle fibres behind the gut contract to make the passageway narrower, forcing the contents along. This circular contraction gradually moves along the tract, pushing the contents ahead of it. At the same time lengthways or longitudinal muscle fibres shorten in front of the contents, to pull the gut backwards past the contents.

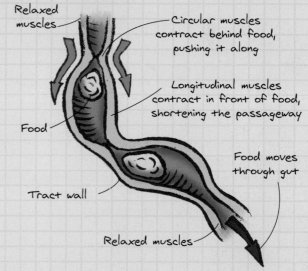

Relaxed muscles

Circular muscles contract behind food, pushing it along

Longitudinal muscles contract in front of food, shortening the passageway

Food

Food moves through gut

Tract wall

Relaxed muscles

Apart from busy muscles (including the heart), the liver generates most the body's warmth, as it carries out hundreds of chemical actions on foods.

On average, food spends less than one minute being chewed in the mouth and a similar time in the oesophagus, but 2 to 4 hours in the stomach, 4 to 6 hours in the small intestine, and 12 hours or more in the large intestine.

WASTE REMOVAL

Every second, blood collects a huge variety of wastes from the body's chemical processes (metabolism). One is carbon dioxide, expelled from the lungs. Almost all the other wastes are filtered from the blood by the kidneys. Each kidney contains about one million tiny filter units known as nephrons, which are marvels of micro-engineered water disposal and recycling.

Did you know?

To filter wastes efficiently, the kidneys receive a huge supply of blood – far more for their size than other organs. Up to one-quarter of all the blood pumped out from the heart passes through them, so that all the body's blood flows through the kidneys in four or five minutes.

Urine is usual 95 percent water.

URINARY SYSTEM

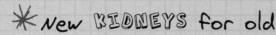

To replace water lost in breath, sweat, faeces and urine, the body should take in at least 2.5 litres daily.

✳ New KIDNEYS for old

In kidney failure, the filtering mechanisms become less efficient and wastes build up in the blood to dangerous levels. One solution is dialysis, where blood is led away from the body along a tube and through a machine that carries out most of the filtering functions. This usually takes 2–3 hours, 2–3 times each week. In peritoneal dialysis, fluid is put into the abdomen (stomach) through a tube, usually for several hours a day, to soak up or absorb the wastes, and is then drained away. A long term solution is a kidney transplant, which can last 20 years or more.

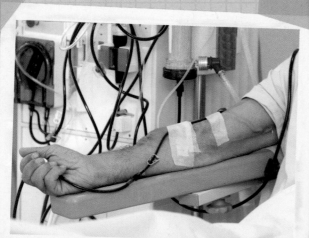

Dialysis replicates many functions of the kidneys

Blood supply The renal artery, which takes blood to the kidney, and the renal vein, which takes away cleaned blood, are short but very wide.

Kidneys The left kidney is slightly higher than the right one. Both are in the upper rear of the abdomen, near the backbone.

Ureter Urine from the kidney passes along the narrow, muscular ureter tube to the bladder. The urine is propelled by peristaltic waves, similar to those that move food in the digestive system.

Bladder This muscle-walled bag can expand gradually to hold more urine. To release the contents, a muscular ring called the urinary sphincter relaxes at the start of its exit tube, the urethra.

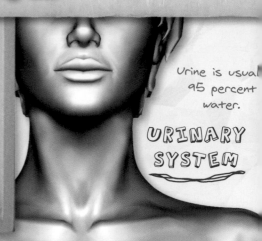
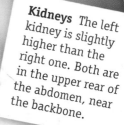

Read more about how kidneys filter blood and keep your body balanced by visiting www.factsforprojects.com and clicking on the web link.

INSIDE A KIDNEY

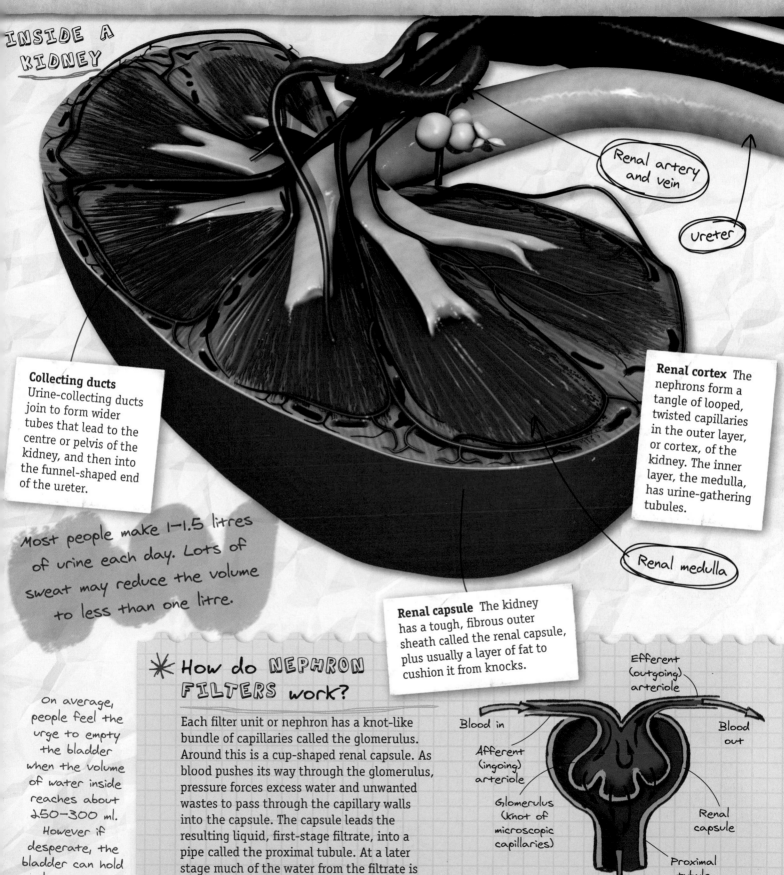

Renal artery and vein

Ureter

Collecting ducts Urine-collecting ducts join to form wider tubes that lead to the centre or pelvis of the kidney, and then into the funnel-shaped end of the ureter.

Renal cortex The nephrons form a tangle of looped, twisted capillaries in the outer layer, or cortex, of the kidney. The inner layer, the medulla, has urine-gathering tubules.

Renal medulla

Most people make 1–1.5 litres of urine each day. Lots of sweat may reduce the volume to less than one litre.

Renal capsule The kidney has a tough, fibrous outer sheath called the renal capsule, plus usually a layer of fat to cushion it from knocks.

✳ How do NEPHRON FILTERS work?

On average, people feel the urge to empty the bladder when the volume of water inside reaches about 250–300 ml. However if desperate, the bladder can hold almost twice this amount.

Each filter unit or nephron has a knot-like bundle of capillaries called the glomerulus. Around this is a cup-shaped renal capsule. As blood pushes its way through the glomerulus, pressure forces excess water and unwanted wastes to pass through the capillary walls into the capsule. The capsule leads the resulting liquid, first-stage filtrate, into a pipe called the proximal tubule. At a later stage much of the water from the filtrate is taken back into another capillary system, to concentrate the wastes as urine.

Efferent (outgoing) arteriole

Blood in

Blood out

Afferent (ingoing) arteriole

Glomerulus (knot of microscopic capillaries)

Renal capsule

Proximal tubule

First-stage filtrate

LYMPH SYSTEM

Lymph is a pale fluid that is the body's 'alternative' blood. It has up to twice the volume of blood, but no dedicated pump and no outgoing vessels. It starts as the general fluid that oozes from and around cells, tissues and tubes, propelled slowly by the body's movements and the massaging effect of pulsing blood vessels. Lymph collects in tubes or ducts, passes through nodes or 'glands', and eventually rejoins the blood in the upper chest.

Did you know?

Lymph has no special way of taking up oxygen, as blood does in the lungs. But otherwise its tasks are quite similar to blood, including delivery of nutrients and collecting wastes. In particular, lymph has an important role in fighting disease. If an infection strikes, its white blood cell numbers can go up by more than 1000 times.

There are about 500 lymph nodes or 'glands' in a typical human body.

Cervical lymph nodes in neck

Main lymph ducts Smaller lymph vessels gather to form large lymph ducts in the chest and empty the lymph into large veins near the heart.

Axillary lymph nodes These are the nodes in the armpits. Like the cervical nodes in the neck, their tenderness and swelling is often an early sign of a developing infection.

Lymphoid tissues Collections of germ-fighting lymphoid tissues are found in several areas, including the nose and throat (see tonsils, opposite), and lumps called Peyer's patches along the intestine.

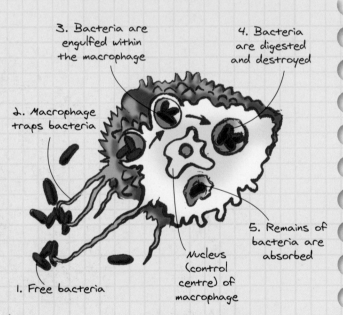

3. Bacteria are engulfed within the macrophage

4. Bacteria are digested and destroyed

2. Macrophage traps bacteria

5. Remains of bacteria are absorbed

Nucleus (control centre) of macrophage

1. Free bacteria

✳ How do WHITE BLOOD CELLS work?

There are several kinds of white blood cell, each with different tasks in defending the body. Macrophages or 'big eaters' consume germs such as bacteria, which are much smaller than them. The macrophage is flexible and puts out long arm-like 'feelers' to search for germs. Any that are found are pulled towards the main cell body, which flows around them to engulf them. Slowly, digestive substances dissolve away the germs. One macrophage can eat more than 100 bacteria during its lifetime of a few months.

To discover more about the lymphatic system and see some brilliant pictures visit www.factsforprojects.com and click on the web link.

The 'adenoids' (pharyngeal tonsils) are lymph-rich tissues at the lower rear of the nasal chamber. The 'tonsils' (palatine tonsils) are similar lumpy tissues in the upper throat.

Adenoids

Tonsils

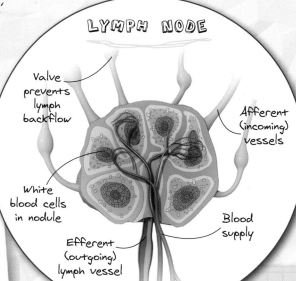

LYMPH NODE

Valve prevents lymph backflow

Afferent (incoming) vessels

White blood cells in nodule

Efferent (outgoing) lymph vessel

Blood supply

If the body is exercising hard, it may call upon the extra blood stored in the spleen. As muscle contractions squeeze this blood into circulation, there may be a sharp pain in the spleen area called a 'stitch'.

Inside a lymph node
Each node has several ducts coming in and just one leaving. It contains smaller nodules inside its strong outer capsule. White cells gather in the cortex and other spaces within the nodules.

Some of the 'memory' white cells in the lymph and immune (self defence) system that recognize germs are almost as old as the body itself.

Spleen In the upper left abdomen behind the stomach, the spleen is the largest lymph organ. It recycles old red blood cells and also stores blood.

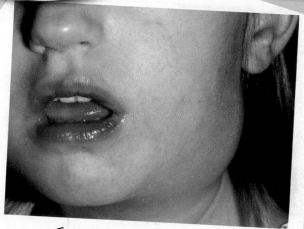

Sometimes when we get an infection our 'glands' swell up

There are usually about 5000–15,000 white blood cells in one pinhead-sized droplet of blood. There are many more red cells — generally around 5 million in the same droplet.

Smallest lymph vessels in fingers

✳ Down in the MOUTH

When the body battles an infection, much of the action takes place in the lymph nodes – commonly called 'glands'. These become centres of germ warfare as white blood cells amass to attack, engulf, disable and destroy invading microbes (see opposite). The dead germs and white cells accumulate and burst open, releasing their fluids. All of these processes make the lymph nodes swell to perhaps five times their healthy size, becoming hot and tender, and sometimes very painful.

HORMONES AND GLANDS

The brain and nerves are one of the body's two control and coordination systems. The other is the hormonal or endocrine system. This uses substances called hormones made in endocrine glands. Most hormones take effect over long periods, from hours to years. They control energy use, levels of minerals and other blood substances, as well as growth and development.

Did you know?

Many hormones work in a 'push-pull' way, with one opposing another to produce finely balanced control. The hormone calcitonin, from the thyroid gland, reduces blood levels of calcium, while parathyroid hormone from the parathyroid glands increases its level.

Pituitary gland Just beneath the lower front of the brain, the pituitary makes about ten hormones. Some of these control the actions of other hormone glands. Pituitary growth hormone affects the whole body.

In 1922, medical workers Frederick Banting and Charles Best showed how injections of insulin could treat the condition of diabetes. Their work has saved millions of lives.

Liver makes three hormones

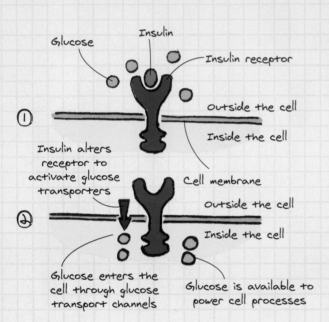

Glucose
Insulin
Insulin receptor
Outside the cell
Inside the cell
①
Insulin alters receptor to activate glucose transporters
Cell membrane
Outside the cell
②
Inside the cell
Glucose enters the cell through glucose transport channels
Glucose is available to power cell processes

Kidneys The hormone renin from the kidney has widespread affects on the amounts of fluids in the body, especially how much water they contain. In this way it controls the amounts of urine produced and also affects blood pressure.

Adrenaline from the adrenal glands is one of the fastest-acting hormones, causing effects in just a few seconds.

 ## How do HORMONES work?

Most hormones seem to work using receptors that are sited in the outer 'skins' or membranes of microscopic cells. The hormone particle or molecule slots into its specially shaped receptor like a key fitting in a lock. This alters the shape of the receptor and triggers further actions. For example, the hormone insulin fits into its receptors in the membranes of certain cells. This activates channel-like gateways further along the cell membrane, allowing in high-energy glucose molecules, to be stored or to drive various life processes within the cell.

Sex hormones In females (shown here), the ovaries produce hormones such as oestrogen and progesterone, which control egg release and the reproductive cycle. The male testes make testosterone, which stimulates sperm development.

To find out more about the hormones in your body and what they do visit www.factsforprojects.com and click on the web link.

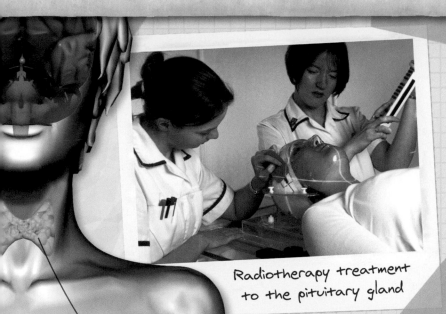

Radiotherapy treatment to the pituitary gland

✳ HORMONE trouble

Rarely, hormonal glands become under- or overactive, perhaps because they develop a growth or tumour. An overactive thyroid gland produces too much thyroxine, which makes chemical processes through the whole body speed up. This is known as hyperthyroidism and the person becomes nervous and anxious, and loses weight. If the thyroid gland is underactive, in hypothyroidism, the body becomes slow and lethargic, lacking energy. These types of problems can usually be treated with medical drugs, surgery, or radiotherapy (X-rays or similar) to shrink the growth.

Thyroid and parathyroid glands In the front of the neck, the thyroid releases thyroxine. This controls the speed at which cells around the body take in energy and carry out their internal processes.

The hormone melatonin from the brain's pineal gland controls our sleep-wake cycle.

Adrenal gland on top of kidney

Adrenal gland The adrenal is really two glands in one. Hormones from its cortex affect water and mineral balance, and how the body copes with stress. The hormone adrenaline from its medulla activates the 'fight-or-flight' response.

Pancreas Insulin and glucagon, both produced in this gland, control the level of blood glucose by a 'push-pull' system.

Uterus (womb) Hormones control pregnancy and birth. During labour, the hormone oxytocin makes the uterus contract, then instructs the body to release milk. It even helps the mother to bond with her baby.

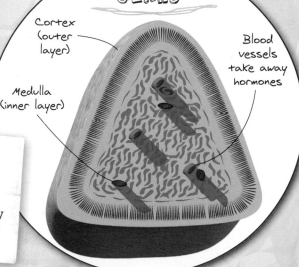

ADRENAL GLAND

Cortex (outer layer)

Medulla (inner layer)

Blood vessels take away hormones

EYES AND SIGHT

For most people, sight is the dominant sense. It brings almost as much information into the brain as all the other senses combined. The eyes can be regarded as outgrowths of the brain. With 120 million-plus light-detecting cells each, they can see clear detail, a wide range of colours, and perceive depth or distance, giving 3D vision.

Did you know?

The six eyeball-moving muscles are among the hardest-working and fastest-reacting in the body. As we watch a speeding object go past, the eyes do not follow it smoothly. They scan it in less than one-tenth of a second, flick sideways to where it will be in another split second, scan it there, and so on – all under automatic brain control.

A jelly-like fluid called vitreous humour fills the eyeball and gives it shape. It is one of the clearest, most transparent substances known.

Optic nerve from eye to brain

Almost all babies are born with bluish eyes. The eventual colour takes a few months to develop.

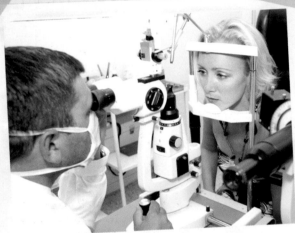

An optician using equipment to give an eye test

✳ It's all CLEAR now

In some people the lens is slightly too weak or strong for the eyeball, or the eyeball itself is slightly over- or under-sized. This results in blurred vision. The solution is an extra lens in front of the body's own one to help with focusing. The extra lens may be a small contact lens on the cornea, or a bigger lens in glasses. In some cases the cornea itself can be sculpted to the correct shape by 'melting' away parts of it with a very precisely aimed laser beam – the cornea soon recovers.

Eye-moving muscles
Also called the extrinsic eye muscles, these are strap-shaped and curve around the eyeball. They anchor at the rear inside of the eye socket, or orbit.

Even when we sleep, the eyeballs flick around as though watching a scene. This is REM, rapid eye movement or 'dreaming' sleep.

Choroid (blood supply layer)

The retina's rod cells see only black and white, but work well in dim conditions. The cones detect colours and fine detail, but need bright conditions to function.

Test your vision with lots of fun activities by visiting
www.factsforprojects.com and clicking on the web link.

Superior eye-moving muscle

Fovea (yellow spot) This is the area where an image focuses for us to see it most clearly, with lots of cone cells.

Ciliary muscles and lens The lens hangs in a circle of ciliary muscles. When these contract they allow the lens to bulge and focus on nearby objects. Relaxed, they make the lens thinner for seeing distant objects.

✳ How does the IRIS control light levels?

In the middle of the iris is what looks like a black spot. In fact it is a hole, the pupil, which lets light rays into the eye. When light levels are low, the iris muscles alter the iris shape to make the pupil larger, or dilated. This means more light rays can enter the eye for a clearer view. In bright conditions the muscles change the iris shape to shrink or constrict the pupil to prevent too much light from damaging the delicate retina. These reflex changes also alter the distance range, or depth of field, which we can see clearly.

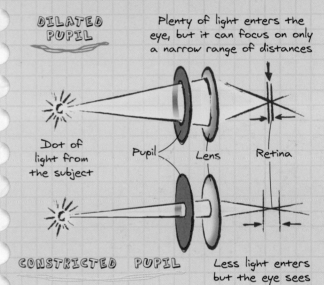

DILATED PUPIL

Plenty of light enters the eye, but it can focus on only a narrow range of distances

Dot of light from the subject

Pupil   Lens   Retina

CONSTRICTED PUPIL

Less light enters but the eye sees a bigger range of distances clearly

Iris The coloured part of the eye, the iris, is a collar-like ring of two sets of muscles. These contract in opposition to alter its size.

Cornea (clear domed front of eye)

The detailed pattern of streaks, pigments and blood vessels on the iris is unique in every eye. Iris scans can be more useful than fingerprints since they are very difficult to fake.

Retina This inner layer contains more than 100 million rod cells and six million cone cells, which turn patterns of light rays into nerve signals.

Sclera The sclera is the tough, pale outermost coating, or sheath, of the eyeball. At the front it is seen as the 'white' of the eye.

EARS AND HEARING

Like sight, hearing is an 'at a-distance' sense. It tells us what is happening away from the body, and gives us warning of approaching dangers such as speeding traffic. The ear flap on the side of the head may look important, but it is only a funnel-shaped guide for invisible sound waves to the inner parts of the ear. The vital process of turning sound vibrations into nerve signals happens in these inner parts.

Did you know?

Sound travels through air at about 340 metres per second. So a sound coming from the side reaches one ear a fraction of a second before the other (and is louder in the first ear too). The time difference is less than 1/1500th of a second – but the brain can detect it.

Temple skin

Skull bone

If the ear detects very loud sounds, in a split second the tiny stapedius muscle attached to the stirrup bone contracts to damp down its vibrations, and prevent damage to the cochlea.

Outer ear (pinna) This collects more sound waves from in front than behind. By comparing volume or loudness, the brain can work out where the sounds come from.

Entrance to ear canal

Ear structure The outer ear flap has an inner framework of bendy cartilage (gristle). It can flex if knocked or rubbed, rather than breaking, as bone might.

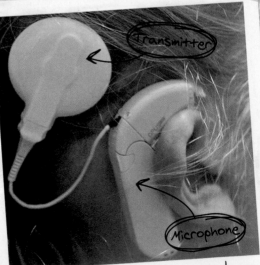

Transmitter

Microphone

A person fitted with a cochlear implant wears a microphone and a transmitter

✳ Loud and CLEAR

Treatments for hearing problems depend on the cause. In conductive problems the sound vibrations have trouble reaching the cochlea in the inner ear. One solution is a hearing aid on or in the ear flap, to boost incoming sounds, make their vibrations larger, and aim them at the eardrum. Some hearing problems are based in the cochlea itself. One answer is an electronic microchip called a cochlear implant that detects vibrations, turns them into tiny electrical signals, and feeds them directly into the nerve to the brain.

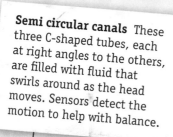

To read more about how ears work and how they help us balance visit www.factsforprojects.com and click on the web link.

Semi circular canals These three C-shaped tubes, each at right angles to the others, are filled with fluid that swirls around as the head moves. Sensors detect the motion to help with balance.

The hair cells in the cochlea are arranged in two long rows, inner and outer, to help us distinguish the volume and pitch of sounds. There are between 15,000 and 20,000 hair cells in each cochlea.

Vestibular nerve from balance organs

Cochlea This snail-shaped organ changes the vibrations of sounds into patterns of nerve signals to send to the brain.

Eustachian tube to throat

Eardrum

Ear bones A chain of three tiny bones, the ear ossicles, link the eardrum to the cochlea. They are called the hammer, anvil and stirrup. They pass along vibrations caused by sound waves hitting the eardrum, also making them more forceful.

Middle ear space The tiny ossicle bones bridge the air-filled middle ear between the eardrum and cochlea, held in place by minute, delicate ligaments and tendons.

Humans can hear sound pitches between about 20 and 20,000 vibrations per second. Dolphins and bats can hear up to 200,000.

✳ How do we HEAR?

Sound waves are areas of high and low pressure travelling through the air. They hit the eardrum and make it vibrate. The vibrations pass along the ear bones to the cochlea, causing similar waves of high and low pressure to ripple through the fluid inside. The ripples shake a flexible flap called the tectorial membrane. In this are embedded the tips of microscopic hairs from thousands of hair cells arranged in a spiral strip, the organ of Corti. When the tectorial membrane shakes, the hairs do too, and stimulate the hair cells to make nerve signals. Different parts of the membrane shake for low- or high-pitched sounds.

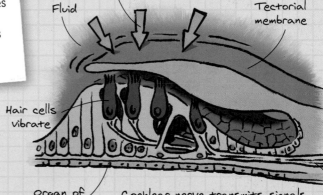

Sound waves in the cochlear fluid cause the tectorial membrane to vibrate

Fluid

Tectorial membrane

Hair cells vibrate

Organ of Corti

Cochlear nerve transmits signals from the hair cells to the brain

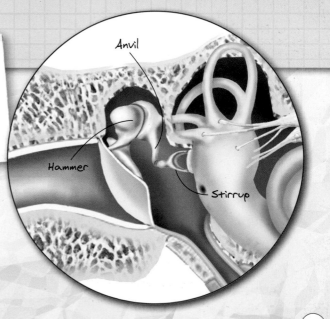

Anvil

Hammer

Stirrup

TASTE AND SMELL

A delicious meal brings the pleasure of lovely odours and excellent flavours. On the other hand, food that has gone 'off' or is rotten makes us wrinkle our noses and grimace in disgust. The nose at the entrance to the breathing system, and the tongue at the start of the digestive system, give early warning about foul air or putrid tastes, so we can take action to avoid them. These two senses work in similar ways, by detecting tiny particles or molecules of smells and flavours.

Did you know?

Smell is far more sensitive than taste. The nose can distinguish more than 10,000 different scents, odours and aromas. The tongue picks up only about five basic flavours. However, it does register differing proportions of these in various foods and drinks.

The five basic taste flavours are sweet, salty, sour, bitter and savoury (umami).

Corpus callosum (connects two sides of brain)

Olfactory bulb This mass of nerve cells (see opposite) connects to the hair cells below.

Young people have up to 10,000 taste buds. Older people may have only 5000 — one reason why foods taste more bland with age.

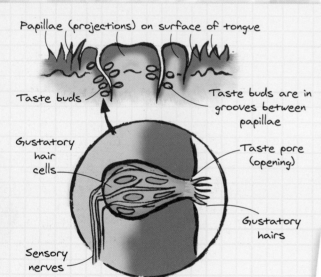

Papillae (projections) on surface of tongue

Taste buds

Taste buds are in grooves between papillae

Gustatory hair cells

Taste pore (opening)

Gustatory hairs

Sensory nerves

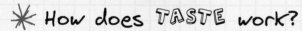

Olfactory epithelium hair cells The smell hair cells (see opposite) work when certain flavour substances touch them.

✳ How does TASTE work?

Taste is based in small clusters of microscopic cells called gustatory hair cells. These work in a similar way to olfactory hair cells (see opposite). The information for tastes is carried by different shapes of substances in food and drinks, known as flavourants. As we eat, these flavourants come into contact with micro-hairs sticking out from the hair cells. If certain types of flavourants fit into corresponding receptors on a micro-hair, the hair cell is triggered to make a nerve signal. In the nose, olfactory hair cells detect floating particles in the air called odourants.

Tongue surface Taste buds are mainly along the sides of the tongue and at its tip and upper rear. There are very few in the middle of the upper surface.

Tongue muscle fibres

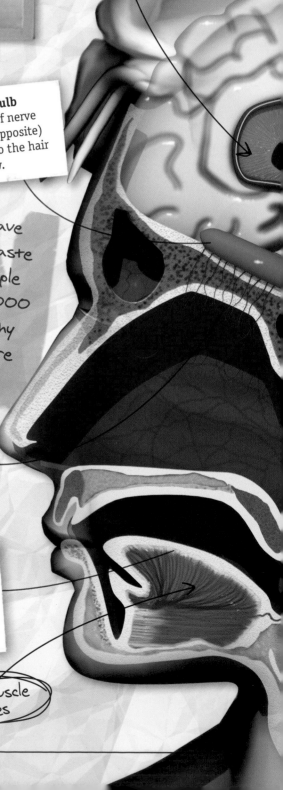

To test your sense of taste against your sense of smell visit www.factsforprojects.com and click on the web link.

Ventricles The brain is partly hollow. Inside are fluid-filled chambers called ventricles. The cerebrospinal fluid in them helps to distribute nutrients and collect waste.

There are more than 40 million olfactory hair cells in the nose. Some dogs have ten times as many.

Inside the olfactory bulb Nerve signals from the olfactory hair cells are compared, analyzed and 'pre-sorted' before passing along the olfactory tract to the brain.

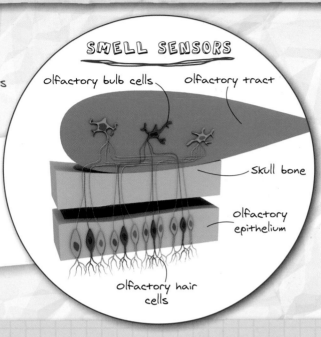

SMELL SENSORS

olfactory bulb cells

olfactory tract

Skull bone

olfactory epithelium

olfactory hair cells

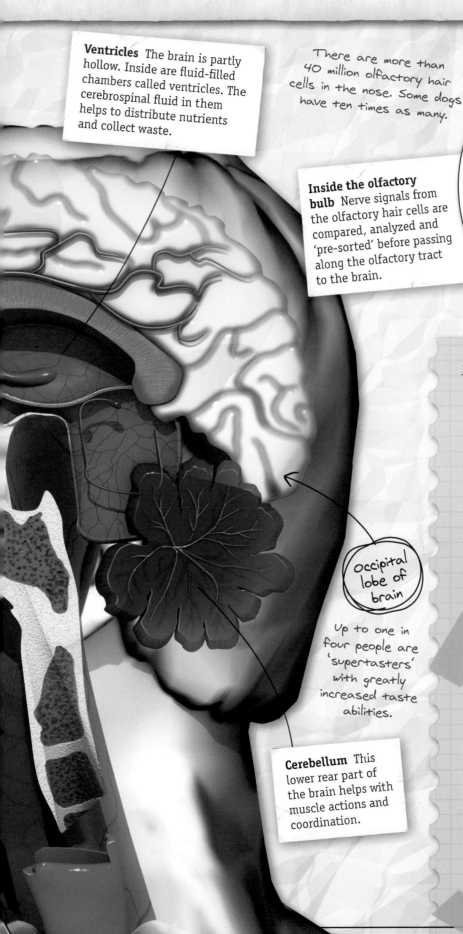

Occipital lobe of brain

Up to one in four people are 'supertasters' with greatly increased taste abilities.

Cerebellum This lower rear part of the brain helps with muscle actions and coordination.

✳ Lip SMACKING!

The enjoyment of 'tasty' foods is based largely on smell. As we eat, the taste buds detect flavours on the tongue. But chewing the food also releases many aromas that waft from the back of the mouth, around the gap at the rear of the palate (roof of the mouth)and up into the nasal chamber. Here they are sensed in great detail by the olfactory epithelium. Taste and smell are separate senses, but as we eat, the brain receives masses of information from both. It comes to associate the odours with the flavours, creating an overall 'taste sensation'.

Taste combines with sensations such as temperature

BRAIN AND NERVES

Everything associated with the mind and consciousness – thoughts, memories, feelings, emotions, urges, even daydreams – is based in the brain. Despite its appearance, this greyish-pink, unmoving organ is one of the body's busiest. Its 'language' is tiny electrical nerve signals. Every second, millions of them arrive from the senses, flash around the brain, and go out to the muscles.

Did you know?

The average brain weighs 1400 grams, which is 1/50th of body weight. But the brain is so active that it consumes up to one-fifth of all the energy used by the body. The energy is brought by the blood, usually as glucose (blood sugar). A lack of this for just a few seconds can cause problems.

The brain's electrical nerve signals are recorded as an EEG, electro-encephalogram.

Touch centre for skin

Brain map This artificial coloured view of the brain shows how different parts of its outer surface, the cerebral cortex, are important in different tasks. Brown shows the area assisting vision.

Our brains allow us to draw from memory, expressing emotions

occipital lobe

Vision area The lower rear of the brain receives and analyzes nerve messages from the eyes, and gives us perception of what we see.

✳ ARTISTIC flair

Where do ideas and creative skills come from? In most people, the brain shares out certain tasks between its two halves. The left side or cerebral hemisphere is mainly concerned with rational thought, logic, and mental activities such as calculations, breaking things down into parts and step-by-step reasoning. The right side takes the lead in inventive thinking, jumping towards whole ideas, linking random thoughts, and appreciation of art and music. Suitable types of 'brain training' can help people to involve both sides of the brain when tackling an activity, often with a better overall result.

Cerebellum This lower wrinkled part coordinates motor nerve signals going out to the muscles, to make movements smooth, skilled and precisely controlled.

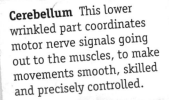

There is no link, in otherwise healthy people, between brain size and intelligence.

Spinal cord (main nerve to body)

Navigate around an interactive brain and learn more about its functions by visiting www.factsforprojects.com and clicking on the web link.

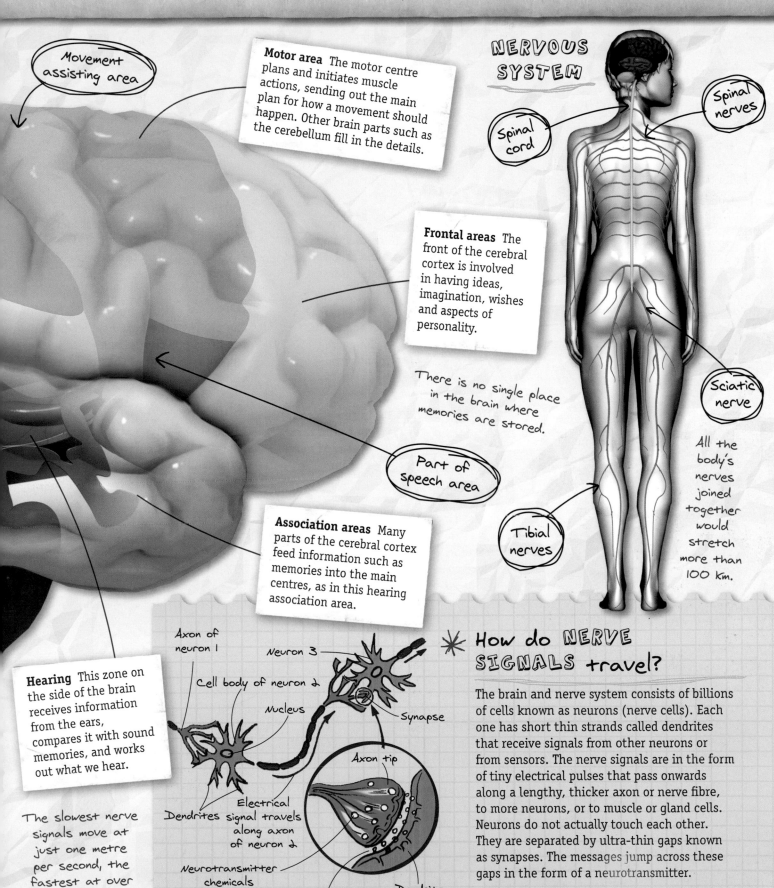

Movement assisting area

Motor area The motor centre plans and initiates muscle actions, sending out the main plan for how a movement should happen. Other brain parts such as the cerebellum fill in the details.

NERVOUS SYSTEM

Spinal cord

Spinal nerves

Frontal areas The front of the cerebral cortex is involved in having ideas, imagination, wishes and aspects of personality.

There is no single place in the brain where memories are stored.

Part of speech area

Sciatic nerve

All the body's nerves joined together would stretch more than 100 km.

Association areas Many parts of the cerebral cortex feed information such as memories into the main centres, as in this hearing association area.

Tibial nerves

Hearing This zone on the side of the brain receives information from the ears, compares it with sound memories, and works out what we hear.

The slowest nerve signals move at just one metre per second, the fastest at over 100.

Axon of neuron 1

Neuron 3

Cell body of neuron 2

Nucleus

Synapse

Axon tip

Dendrites

Electrical signal travels along axon of neuron 2

Neurotransmitter chemicals

Synaptic gap

Dendrite

* How do NERVE SIGNALS travel?

The brain and nerve system consists of billions of cells known as neurons (nerve cells). Each one has short thin strands called dendrites that receive signals from other neurons or from sensors. The nerve signals are in the form of tiny electrical pulses that pass onwards along a lengthy, thicker axon or nerve fibre, to more neurons, or to muscle or gland cells. Neurons do not actually touch each other. They are separated by ultra-thin gaps known as synapses. The messages jump across these gaps in the form of a neurotransmitter.

GLOSSARY

Abdomen
The lower part of the main body (torso) that contains organs for digestion, waste removal and, in females, reproduction.

Alveoli
Microscopic air chambers in the lungs where oxygen passes into the blood by flowing through capillaries.

Artery
A blood vessel that carries blood away from the heart.

Axon
The long, thin part of a nerve cell or neuron that carries away nerve signals to pass them on to other nerve cells or to muscles. Also called a nerve fibre.

Bronchi
The main airways in the lungs that lead from the trachea (windpipe) deep into the lung tissues.

Canines
Long, sharp teeth near the front of the mouth, used for jabbing and stabbing.

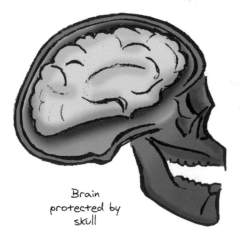

Brain protected by skull

Capillaries
The smallest blood vessels in the body, which allow oxygen and nutrients to pass from the blood into the surrounding cells and tissues. Carbon dioxide and wastes can move the opposite way into the blood.

Cartilage
A strong but slightly flexible body substance, less stiff than bone that forms parts of the skeleton and also covers bones inside joints.

Cerebellum
The lower rear part of the brain, which co-ordinates the nerve signals going out to muscles.

Cochlea
The coiled part deep in the ear that changes the patterns of sound rays that vibrate it into patterns of nerve signals to send to the brain.

Cornea
The domed, clear front of the eye, through which light rays pass and are part-focused, before they go through the lens behind it for fine focusing.

Cortex
The outer layer of an organ such as the kidney or adrenal gland, usually distinct from its inner layer, the medulla.

Dendrites
The short, thin parts of a nerve cell or neuron that gather nerve signals from other cells.

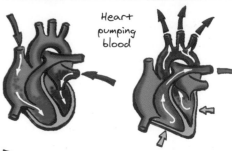

Heart pumping blood

Diaphragm
A sheet of muscle at the base of the lungs between the chest and abdomen. When it contracts, the diaphragm powers the movements of breathing.

Diastole
The phase of the heartbeat when the heart muscles relax and its chambers expand as they refill with blood from the veins.

Glucose
Blood sugar, a type of sugar that contains lots of energy in chemical form. It is obtained from digestion and carried in the blood for use as a general energy source all around the body.

Gluteus maximus
The main muscle in the hip and upper leg which provides the power for movement, such as walking and running.

Gustatory hair cells
Microscopic, smell-sensitive cells inside taste buds that detect flavour particles in foods and drinks, and generate corresponding patterns of nerve signals to send to the brain.

Hormones
Chemical substances made in endocrine glands, which travel in the blood and affect certain parts of the body – the targets – controlling the activity of their cells and tissues.

Incisors

Teeth at the front of the mouth, usually sharp and straight-edged, used for nibbling and gnawing.

Iris

The coloured ring of muscle at the front of the eye that adjusts the size of the hole at its centre, the pupil, according to light levels.

Large intestine

Part of the gut, usually short and wide that absorbs water, vitamins and minerals from digested food, and converts the remains into waste, ready for removal as faeces.

Ligaments

Strong straps that hold together the bones in a joint, so they do not dislocate (come apart or slip out of position).

Lungs

Body parts specialized to take in oxygen from the air and pass it to the blood. Lungs also get rid of waste carbon dioxide from the blood, out into the air.

Mandible

The lower jaw.

Molars

The broad, strong teeth towards the back of the mouth, used for crushing and chewing.

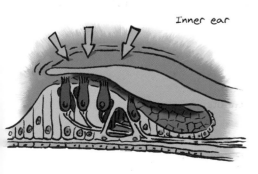

Inner ear

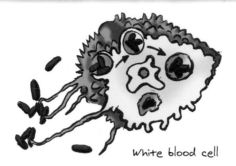

White blood cell

Medulla

The inner layer of an organ such as the kidney or adrenal gland, usually distinct from its outer layer, the cortex.

Nephrons

The microscopic filter units in a kidney, each consisting of a network of capillaries and other tubes that remove wastes and excess water from the blood.

Neurons

Nerve cells that receive, analyze, co-ordinate and pass on nerve signals in the form of tiny pulses of electricity. They usually have short projections called dendrites and a longer one, the axon.

Oesophagus

Also called the gullet, the first part of the gut after the mouth and throat leading down to the stomach.

Olfactory hair cells

Microscopic, smell-sensitive cells inside the nose, which detect odour particles floating in the air and generate corresponding patterns of nerve signals to send to the brain.

Pectoralis

The main muscle in the front chest area, which raises and swings the arm.

Pupil

In the eye, the hole in the ring of muscle called the iris. Light passes through the pupil to the lens inside the eyeball.

Retina

The light-sensitive layer inside the eyeball that changes the patterns of light rays falling on it into corresponding patterns of nerve signals to send to the brain.

Skeleton

The strong supporting framework inside the body, made of 206 bones plus some cartilage.

Small intestine

Part of the gut that is long, thin and coiled, and absorbs nutrients from digested food, into the blood.

Systole

The phase of the heartbeat when the heart muscles contract powerfully to squeeze blood out into the arteries.

Taste buds

Microscopic bundles of cells on the tongue that detect flavour particles in foods and drinks.

Tendons

Strong, tough, rope-like parts that join muscles to bones.

Vein

A blood vessel that carries blood towards the heart.

Vertebrae

Backbones, the long chain of linked bones that make up the spinal column, often called the backbone.

INDEX